Samuel French Acting Edition

View of the Dome

by Theresa Rebeck

SAMUELFRENCH.COM   SAMUELFRENCH.CO.UK

Copyright © 1998 by Madwoman in the Attic
All Rights Reserved

VIEW OF THE DOME is fully protected under the copyright laws of the United States of America, the British Commonwealth, including Canada, and all other countries of the Copyright Union. All rights, including professional and amateur stage productions, recitation, lecturing, public reading, motion picture, radio broadcasting, television and the rights of translation into foreign languages are strictly reserved.

ISBN 978-0-573-62603-6

www.SamuelFrench.com
www.SamuelFrench.co.uk

FOR PRODUCTION ENQUIRIES

UNITED STATES AND CANADA
Info@SamuelFrench.com
1-866-598-8449

UNITED KINGDOM AND EUROPE
Plays@SamuelFrench.co.uk
020-7255-4302

Each title is subject to availability from Samuel French, depending upon country of performance. Please be aware that *VIEW OF THE DOME* may not be licensed by Samuel French in your territory. Professional and amateur producers should contact the nearest Samuel French office or licensing partner to verify availability.

CAUTION: Professional and amateur producers are hereby warned that *VIEW OF THE DOME* is subject to a licensing fee. Publication of this play(s) does not imply availability for performance. Both amateurs and professionals considering a production are strongly advised to apply to Samuel French before starting rehearsals, advertising, or booking a theatre. A licensing fee must be paid whether the title(s) is presented for charity or gain and whether or not admission is charged. Professional/Stock licensing fees are quoted upon application to Samuel French.

No one shall make any changes in this title(s) for the purpose of production. No part of this book may be reproduced, stored in a retrieval system, or transmitted in any form, by any means, now known or yet to be invented, including mechanical, electronic, photocopying, recording, videotaping, or otherwise, without the prior written permission of the publisher. No one shall upload this title(s), or part of this title(s), to any social media websites.

For all enquiries regarding motion picture, television, and other media rights, please contact Samuel French.

MUSIC USE NOTE

Licensees are solely responsible for obtaining formal written permission from copyright owners to use copyrighted music in the performance of this play and are strongly cautioned to do so. If no such permission is obtained by the licensee, then the licensee must use only original music that the licensee owns and controls. Licensees are solely responsible and liable for all music clearances and shall indemnify the copyright owners of the play(s) and their licensing agent, Samuel French, against any costs, expenses, losses and liabilities arising from the use of music by licensees. Please contact the appropriate music licensing authority in your territory for the rights to any incidental music.

IMPORTANT BILLING AND CREDIT REQUIREMENTS

If you have obtained performance rights to this title, please refer to your licensing agreement for important billing and credit requirements.

VIEW OF THE DOME was originally produced in New York by The New York Theatre Workshop on September 13, 1996. It was directed by Michael Mayer. The cast was as follows:

SENATOR GEOFFREY MADDOX	Jim Abele
TOMMY	Patrick Breen
ANNABETH GILKEY	Candy Buckley
E.T. BLACK	Tom Riis Farrell
EMMA	Julia Gibson
DAVID	Dion Graham
ARTHUR WOOLF	Richard Poe

The scenic design was by Neil Patel; costume design by Michael Krass; lighting design by Frances Aronson; sound design by Darron L. West. The production stage manager was Lisa Lacucci and the assistant stage manager was Charles Means.

(A restaurant. Two tables. One seats four people in a lively debate. At the second, a single woman sits alone.)

ANNABETH. I was mentioning to the senator what an extraordinary coincidence -- is this vinagarette? I don't think this is the vinagarette.
TOMMY. No, that's it --
ANNABETH. Are you sure?
ARTHUR. Yes, I've got the same thing. It's a raspberry --
ANNABETH. But this looks like it has cream in it.
TOMMY. No, I don't think so --
ANNABETH. In any event, I was telling the senator how extraordinary I thought it was, when I heard Arthur speaking about the call to public service, how close your two positions actually are, and how rare it is to hear politicians, even aspiring politicians, actually speak of civic duty --
SENATOR. Yes, I think the last time someone even said the words up on the hill they were quietly taken aside and stoned.

(They all laugh.)

ANNABETH. Exactly. So I said to Arthur, you have to meet the Senator and tell him your ideas. But when you get to the part about "civic duty" -- keep your voice down.

(They all laugh again. The laughter stops suddenly as EMMA raises her eyes and speaks to the audience.)

EMMA. Do any of you find this interesting? Some of you must. Every night of the week, all across America, near strangers who want something from each other gather and enact a social ritual involving food which nobody has to pay for because it's being expensed. And then everyone talks about nothing for a couple of hours, somehow sliding into the cracks the mysterious subject of What They Want, and then everybody goes away, pondering the even more mysterious subject of What They Got. It's called a political dinner.

SENATOR. So, Arthur, you're thinking of taking a run at Congress?

ARTHUR. Well, I'm afraid it's gone a little farther than that. I declared my candidacy last week.

SENATOR. *(Mock dismay)* Oh, dear. Then I've come too late.

(They all laugh again.)

EMMA. I happen to think political dinners are a huge crashing bore. Nevertheless, I would give anything to be sitting at that table.

ANNABETH. Oh, the escargot are excellent. Geoffrey – Senator – I think they're even better than the ones we had in Nice.

SENATOR. The ones *you* had. I'm afraid I'm too much of an American to actually consume a garden slug.

(They laugh.)

EMMA. I walked in with those people.
SENATOR. Are you a snail man, Arthur?

EMMA. In fact, I drove them here.
ARTHUR. Well, I'm afraid –
SENATOR. Careful.
ARTHUR. Absolutely not.
ANNABETH. Oh, stop.

(She feeds him a snail.)

EMMA. You have no idea where this sort of thing can lead. This is what happened. *(She stands and crosses to the table, indicating ARTHUR.)* Two weeks ago, I received a phone call from this man's wife. Her name is Natalie, she and Arthur and I are old friends, and she wants to know if I will have dinner with them tonight.

ARTHUR. The challenge of any society is balancing the rights of the individual against the rights of the community. America, built on the dream of rugged individualism, is directly challenged by communism, which annihilates the individual and promotes only the dream of the community. But just as communism finally destroyed itself, crumbling under the weight of its singular dream, so shall we fall unless we find a way to support a dynamic interchange between self and society.

EMMA. Now, the fact is, I am a sucker for this kind of shit.

ARTHUR. This is the job of a leader. To protect the individual, and the community, at the same time.

EMMA. Arthur was one of my professors in law school. While everyone else was busy grinding my imagination to smithereens, Arthur spoke of –

ANNABETH. Dreams! Another word you don't hear on the hill ...

SENATOR. They stone you for that too, Arthur.
ARTHUR. Mea culpa, mea culpa!

(They all laugh.)

EMMA. So me, Arthur, and Natalie are going to dinner, when Tommy calls to tell us Annabeth Gilkey has arranged for us to meet Senator Geoffrey Maddox in her office. We planned to hook up with Natalie after, but she gets a head cold and bags the trip.
ANNABETH. He's so delightfully idealistic, isn't he, Geoffrey?
ARTHUR. Oh, I don't –
ANNABETH. No, no, it's charming! Mr. Smith Goes To Washington. It reminds me of you, Geoffrey.
SENATOR. Well, I don't –
ANNABETH. Oh, to a tee! And the time is right for this. Public mood.
SENATOR. You might be –
ANNABETH. Who gives a shit about the presidency, we've gotta take the House back. I mean those fascists on the right are just driving me nuts. Gingrich, and Robertson, those idiot freshmen – oh, my God, Rush Limbaugh, when is he gonna go away.
SENATOR. The situation is difficult right now.
ANNABETH. I know, it's late, the primary is only a couple months away, but let's face it, we've got *no one* who stands a chance and Geoffrey, I'm telling you, I can *do* something with this. And you know I wouldn't say it if it weren't true.

(She smiles at him.)

EMMA. Annabeth Gilkey is living proof that it is in fact possible to sleep your way to the top, in any field. She is the kind of person who, if she owned a fur coat, it would be made of puppies.

(The scene changes to ANNABETH's office. The SENATOR leaves.)

EMMA. We arrive at Annabeth's office fifteen minutes early.
ANNABETH. Emma! How lovely to see you again! I didn't know you were coming.
EMMA. Why wouldn't I be coming?
ARTHUR. Is my tie all right?
EMMA. *(Checking it)* It's fine –
ARTHUR. I'm so nervous –
EMMA. He's gonna love you –
ARTHUR. I just hope I get a chance to explain my ideas to him.
TOMMY. You were great with the governor.
ANNABETH. The governor? Arthur, you *are* moving up quickly.
EMMA. He's a friend of my dad's.
ANNABETH. How darling.
EMMA. Arthur knocked him dead. We're on our way!
ANNABETH. You already have a whole organization, Arthur. What's your title, Emma?
EMMA. *(Fixing tie)* We haven't gotten to that yet.
ARTHUR. Chief of staff.

(They laugh.)

ANNABETH. How darling.

EMMA. Okay, see you guys at the restaurant. Give my best to the senator.

ANNABETH. Actually, the senator's had to postpone.

(There is an awkward, disappointed pause.)

TOMMY. Oh?

ARTHUR. Oh.

ANNABETH. Oh, stop! Such long faces. He's just running late. He's going to join us. Where were you going?

EMMA. Chardonnay.

ANNABETH. Fabulous. *(She picks up the phone and punches a button)* Jennie? It's Annabeth. The Senator asked me to call and let him know where we'd be having dinner. We're heading over to Chardonny, can you let him know? Thanks, you're a doll. *(She hangs up, bright)* Shall we?

(The scene changes back to the restaurant.)

EMMA. *(To audience)* So all of us get into my car and we drive across town, to a very nice, very discreet French restaurant.

ANNABETH. I *love* this place.

EMMA. Where I have made a reservation.

ANNABETH. And I hardly ever get over here.

EMMA. To have dinner with my friends and colleagues.

ANNABETH. Now, how do you want to do the seating, Arthur? Four and one?

(EMMA looks over as ARTHUR considers this.)

ARTHUR. *(Quickly)* Oh, yes. That's exactly right. Four and one.

ANNABETH. David – We'll need a table for four, and a table for one.

DAVID. Right this way.

EMMA. *(To audience)* I wish I could say that it took me a minute to get this, but unfortunately I understood immediately what was going on.

TOMMY. Wait a minute. There are going to be five of us, aren't there? When the senator gets here –

EMMA. *(To TOMMY)* Apparently, Annabeth and Arthur would prefer that I ate at a separate table.

ANNABETH. We'll set you up at the best single they have. David, can we get her the view of the capitol dome?

DAVID. Anything for you, Annabeth.

ARTHUR. Emma, you understand. This is strictly business.

EMMA. Of course!

ARTHUR. The senator –

EMMA. I know.

DAVID. It's a little close to the kitchen and there is a draft, but I think you'll be very pleased with the view.

ARTHUR. *(To ANNABETH)* I can't tell you how much I appreciate your help arranging this, Annabeth –

ANNABETH. I didn't do it for you, Arthur. I did it for all of us. Now, you and Tommy need to fill me in on your campaign strategy before the senator gets here.

ARTHUR. Of course! Tommy –

(They all sit at their respective tables.)

EMMA. *(To audience)* So, they get to work. I order a drink. *(She does. The waiter delivers it.)* The senator arrives. *(He does. The waiter knocks the drink on EMMA in his rush to serve the senator.)* *(More and more rattled)* And while they chat, I eat alone. I don't have a book with me because I didn't realize that I would be eating alone. I don't have a newspaper because, same thing. I don't have anyone to talk to because, well, that's obvious. Plus, the service is terrible because everyone in the restaurant is obsessed with "Geoffrey," the senator, once he gets here. So, I sit alone for two hours, wondering why the hell I went along with this, why Arthur went along with it, why Tommy went along with it, and why the fuck the vinagarette has cream in it!

(Everyone bursts into laughter at the next table. EMMA stabs her salad, eating angrily.)

SENATOR. Oh, look at the time! I'm going to miss that fundraiser altogether.
ANNABETH. Well, maybe you should –
SENATOR. I wish. But I've *got* to put in an appearance. You'll join me, of course.
ARTHUR. That would be delightful –
SENATOR. That's the last time you'll say that, Arthur. If all goes well for you, and I'm sure it will, you will get very tired of fundraisers.
ARTHUR. That's very kind of you.
SENATOR. We'll have to call a cab, I'm afraid. I sent the car ahead with my wife –
ARTHUR. No, no, that's not a problem. We have a car.
SENATOR. Wonderful!

ARTHUR. Yes, we drove down from Baltimore with my dear friend Emma. Emma –

(He brings the SENATOR over to EMMA's table.)

EMMA. Hello! Yes –
ARTHUR. The senator is heading over to that DNC fundraiser. He'd like us to come along.
SENATOR. You came down together? Why didn't you have dinner with us?
EMMA. *(Smiling)* Apparently, I'm not important enough to sit at your table.

(She laughs. They laugh. ARTHUR gives her a hug.)

SENATOR. Certainly not –
ARTHUR. Oh, no, it wasn't that –
ANNABETH. Aren't we heading over? We'd better go soon, or Geoffrey may just turn into a pumpkin. Think of how *that* would look in the morning papers.

(They all laugh again. The scene changes.)

EMMA. What a surprise. The fundraiser is a huge crashing bore. It's just like a political dinner, except the drinks are watered, everyone stands up and for some reason there's a military band ... At times like this, one cannot help but wonder about the rituals of white people.

(The SENATOR exits. Music plays. As before, EMMA stands off to one side.)

ANNABETH. *(Waving, working the room)* Frank, how are you? I *loved* what you said on Nightline the other night. I thought Cokie Roberts was going to *hit* you. Paul, meet Arthur Woolf. Maryland's next congressman from District 2.

TOMMY. Al Gore's here.

SENATOR. Emma! Here you are off in a corner again. I've been looking for you.

EMMA. You have?

SENATOR. Would you like to dance?

EMMA. Here? Now?

SENATOR. With me?

EMMA. Maybe the evening won't be a complete disaster after all. I'd love to.

(The music changes into a tango. EMMA and the SENATOR dance.)

SENATOR. So what do you do, Emma?

EMMA. I'm a lawyer.

SENATOR. Really? My wife is a lawyer.

EMMA. Yes, we've met. I was opposing council on that Bennington suit.

SENATOR. That was you? You really made her work.

EMMA. Not hard enough. She whipped the pants off me.

(The SENATOR dips her.)

SENATOR. Sounds fascinating.

(ANNABETH snaps into action.)

ANNABETH. Arthur, let's dance.

ARTHUR. Shouldn't I be mingling?

ANNABETH. That depends on what kind of a dancer you are. If you're any good at all, this is a much better way to get people talking about you.

(She whips him around and dips him. Very quickly, there are dueling tangos.)

SENATOR. So how do you know Arthur, Emma?

EMMA. He was one of my professors, my first year of law school.

SENATOR. And now you work for him?

EMMA. Unofficially.

SENATOR. Sounds romantic.

EMMA. Arthur? No.

SENATOR. Excellent.

(He dips her again.)

ARTHUR. Don't you think I should put together a policy statement?

ANNABETH. That's a wonderful point, Arthur. The problem is, no one reads policy statements.

ARTHUR. But everyone says they're sick of the status quo. We have to provide people with options.

ANNABETH. Americans are afraid of ideas.

ARTHUR. Then we have to teach them that there's nothing to be afraid of.

ANNABETH. Oh, Arthur. You are just perfect. I can work with this, I really can. *(Suddenly, flashbulbs go off. ARTHUR looks up, startled. ANNABETH smiles for the camera.)* Perfect.

SENATOR. Now, just a minute there. This is perfectly innocent.

(He goes off after the photographers.)

ANNABETH. I'm telling you, Arthur, my way is easier. We're going to be all over the newspapers by Tuesday.

(She follows the SENATOR off. ARTHUR and TOMMY look at each other. ARTHUR heads after ANNABETH.)
(TOMMY helps EMMA up.)

TOMMY. I'm sorry, Em. Arthur gets nervous at these things. He just started; he doesn't know what he's doing yet. I mean, that thing in the restaurant ...
EMMA. *(Dusting herself off)* It wasn't his fault. Annabeth set me up.
TOMMY. Still. He shouldn't have let it happen.
EMMA. Look, it's okay.
TOMMY. You sure?
EMMA. Yes!
TOMMY. You are such a sport. I'll talk to him about it, okay?

(The scene changes. The phone rings. The waiter comes in and sets the phone before her. It stops ringing and ARTHUR steps into the light.)

ARTHUR. Emma, could you call me? I need to talk to you about something.
EMMA. So, not only am I to be humiliated, now I have

VIEW OF THE DOME

to listen to people apologize about it. Might as well get it over with.

ARTHUR. Hello?

EMMA. Arthur. Hi. I'm returning your call.

ARTHUR. Listen, Emma. I wanted to talk to you about that evening in the restaurant.

EMMA. You know, Arthur, let's just forget about it, okay? It was just an awkward situation.

ARTHUR. Yes, it was, and I really feel that I need to say something about it. I mean, I appreciate everything you've done to help this campaign get off the ground, the money you've given, the introduction to the governor, bringing Tommy on board, the fundraisers you've organized, that's been great, but I have to say, I was really upset with you for the way you behaved the other night.

EMMA. What?

ARTHUR. When you said that you weren't important enough to sit at our table, I felt that you were trying to punish me. And I don't appreciate it. I was going to Washington for an extremely important meeting, something you seen to have completely forgotten –

EMMA. I didn't forget –

ARTHUR. It was not appropriate for you to be there!

EMMA. Whoa! Wait a minute –

ARTHUR. Well, now you're upset. I can't talk to you.

EMMA. Yes, I'm upset. You're yelling at me.

ARTHUR. I'm not yelling, I'm making a point!! If you didn't like the seating arrangements, you should have left the restaurant.

EMMA. I was trying not to create a scene –

ARTHUR. Well, you didn't exactly succeed, now did

you? You were an embarrassment and I won't have it. Do you understand me? I won't have it.

(ARTHUR hangs up the phone. TOMMY enters.)

TOMMY. You okay?

EMMA. Arthur seems angry.

TOMMY. I'm really sorry, Em. Arthur's just, he's a little crazy right now, and somehow, it all got kind of unloaded on you.

EMMA. Why? I didn't do anything!

TOMMY. Well, you did say that thing to the senator about not being important enough to sit at his table.

EMMA. That was true! I was invited to dinner, I *drove* everybody there, and then you guys made me sit at another table! I can't believe I drove. I don't know, that just makes it worse somehow. I *drove*.

TOMMY. I know, it's crazy.

EMMA. And I was willing to let it go! I mean, when it was over, I was like, okay, that was awful, but now it's over, time to move on, and then *he* called *me* –

TOMMY. I know. When he told me he was going to do that, I thought, I wouldn't, it's just putting salt in the wound, but ...

EMMA. He told you? I mean, he told you that he was going to call me and scream at me?

TOMMY. Yeah. And I thought, what a bad idea.

(Beat)

EMMA. But you didn't say that. I mean, you didn't tell him not to. Call me.

(Beat)

TOMMY. Look, let's not blow this out of proportion. These things happen early in a campaign. People are nervous. Things just need to settle out. Let me talk to him.

(ANNABETH and ARTHUR enter. The scene changes. EMMA steps to one side and watches.)

ANNABETH. I really don't understand why she's making such a big deal about this. I mean, really. She is not the one running for office here.

TOMMY. I just think her feelings were hurt.

ANNABETH. Her *feelings*? What do her feelings have to do with anything?

TOMMY. She's done a lot for us. And she is a friend.

ANNABETH. If she were truly a friend, she would understand what our priorities are here. I mean, Arthur has better things to do than running around apologizing for some girl's hurt feelings.

ARTHUR. Apologize? Now she expects me to apologize?

TOMMY. No, that's not –

ARTHUR. Is she insane?

TOMMY. Arthur, she's given us money, she introduced you to the governor – she introduced you to me, for crying out loud – she took a leave of absence from her job to help us out –

ARTHUR. That doesn't give her the right to try and take over the entire campaign.

TOMMY. Arthur –

ARTHUR. No, you listen to me. I know you're friends with Emma, and that has put you in an awkward position here. I respect that. But I also ask that you respect me. I cannot let her wounded ego interfere with what I'm trying to do. What's happening here is bigger than that. The country is at sake. If she can't learn to make a few compromises, then she doesn't belong. And if you don't understand that, then you don't belong, either.

(Beat)

TOMMY. No. I do understand.
ARTHUR. Good.
ANNABETH. Look. I think this all just blew out of proportion.
TOMMY. I think that's all I'm really trying to say.
ANNABETH. Of course you are. And Emma has been a big help to you, Arthur, she has! She told me as much.
ARTHUR. Well, yes, but –
ANNABETH. I think we should conserve our resources, The senator seemed quite taken with her. That could be useful in the long run; he can get skittish during a tough campaign. Besides, if she apologizes, there's no reason why she can't come back.
ARTHUR. No. I suppose not. If she apologizes.
ANNABETH. You'll tell her, won't you, Tommy? Come on, Arthur. We don't want to be late for that lunch with 20/20.

(They go. The scene changes.)

EMMA. They want me to what?

TOMMY. Since the senator liked you so much, they think you could be useful. But you have to apologize.

EMMA. And what exactly am I apologizing for?

TOMMY. Well, it's a difficult situation for everyone. You do share responsibility for this, Em. And he's in no position to apologize to you. I want you around. I think you should do it.

(He goes.)

EMMA. I decide to talk to other people. Be an adult. Get a broader perspective. I call my friends. *(Another woman, MARJORIE, sits across from her. They are having lunch. EMMA launches in.)* It's like, Keats, okay? That negative capability thing? Believing in two completely contradictory ideas at the same time, I always thought that was something deeply profound, like the Heisenberg Uncertainty Principle, if you know where that electron is, you cannot know how fast it's going, or, or Kierkegaard, knowing the universe is going to annihilate you and yet embracing the belief in a just God, all of these things, the resonating of opposites, it always seemed so huge to me, and then it turns out it's not that at all. It turns out, it's just a moment in your life, or a person who you thought was one thing who is in fact also its opposite, or not people, maybe, but the things that we yearn for, small tiny things that then make everything else you thought you knew disappear. And I don't know if I can do it. I mean, maybe I did idealize Arthur, but that still doesn't alter the fact that he fell into that whole nasty in-crowd logic so quickly, and I know he wants this badly, but can a dream destroy your ideals? Are integrity and kindness truly the hope of fools? I don't know what to think anymore.

(MARJORIE stares at her, takes a piece of bread. Pause.)

MARJORIE. You remember last year when we were playing Pictionary, and you accused me of cheating?
EMMA. What?
MARJORIE. You did, you accused me of cheating. *(Pause. Insistent)* On New Year's Eve, we were playing Pictionary, and you said, "come on, come on!"
EMMA. Yes?
MARJORIE. I'm just saying, you know, you're not perfect, either. All this talk about integrity? And *you* accused *me*. Of cheating.
EMMA. Marjorie!
MARJORIE. Look, I have a lot of anger in me, okay? And maybe I should have told you at the time, but this is just not easy for me, and my friends just have to learn to accept my anger because, you know, I have a right to express it. My group feels very strongly about this.

(Pause)

EMMA. I decide that maybe friends are not who I should turn to at this time. Maybe a total stranger, a chance encounter, a foreign perspective will help me understand the mysterious workings of the human heart. Like Diogenes, I go in search of an honest man.

(She turns to sit at a bar. There is a drunken man there.)

E.T. BLACK. Okay, here's the thing: I'm, like, do you know who I am? I'm E.T. Black. That doesn't mean anything

VIEW OF THE DOME

to you, does it? E.T. Black. You've never heard of me. Nobody in this whole place knows who I am. But I'm like, the biggest screenwriter in Hollywood. One of the biggest. Any one of my scripts, I could write anything here, right now, on a napkin, and it would get made. I've got an academy award. You think I'm making this up. But it's because you don't know who I am.

EMMA. Well, I don't go to a lot of movies.

E.T. BLACK. What are you talking about? Everybody goes to movies. What, do you just sit at home and let the television like suck your brains out, is that what you do?

EMMA. No, I'm busy, I'm a busy person.

E.T. BLACK. Oh, little Miss Important, is that who you are? Huh? Too important to go to the movies, is that what you're saying?

EMMA. *(Rising to go)* You know, maybe I ...

E.T. BLACK. No, you talk to me! You said you have a question! Well, I have questions, too! Do you know who I am? I'm E.T. Black! I'm the biggest screenwriter in Hollywood! My movies get made! Nobody reads books anymore! They go to see my movies! If this were the nineteenth century or something I'd be Charles Dickens! *City Slickers*? I wrote that. That thing about starting a stampede with a coffee grinder? That was my idea. *Total Nonsense. Harriet the Spy.* I did the final rewrite on that, most of that is mine. I mean, I'm filthy rich, I'm fuckin' ... filthy rich, and nobody asks me what I think about anything. If this were the nineteenth century, I'd be hanging out with Ruskin. Fucking Ruskin would be having lunch with me. Disraeli. Winston Churchill.

EMMA. Winston Churchill was World War II.

E.T. BLACK. What?

EMMA. Well, you said, if this was the nineteenth century, and Winston Churchill didn't live in the nineteenth century, he –

E.T. BLACK. Fuck you! Do you know who I am? You have no idea who I am!

EMMA. Do you think people are good?

E.T. BLACK. Have you been to Hollywood? No. The answer to that is no.

EMMA. Do you think a dream can destroy ideals?

E.T. BLACK. Ideals? What the fuck is an ideal? Who are you, anyway? Ideals are like, nothing. Fucking Plato forgot to tell you that part. I mean, I thought we were talking about reality. Jesus. You are really sad, lady.

EMMA. We're not talking about me.

E.T. BLACK. No? No? I mean, you wanted the truth, you just, now you don't like it, is that it? I mean, I didn't make this shit up. Do you know who I am? I'm a fuckin' world-famous screenwriter, and I'm telling you the way things are. There are things I *know*. Power and money are *it*. Because people aren't just afraid of death, they're *mad* about it, death is what drives us insane, and we thing if we collect enough ... you know ... *(He starts to drift off.)* Maybe ... if we have enough ... if we're whores ... you know, fucking ... if we live without meaning ... we can beat God at his own fucking game ...

(His head is on the table. EMMA watches him for a moment.)

EMMA. I don't know why it took Diogenes so long to find an honest man. I got one my first time out. I gotta get away from all this. Far away. Alaska. I'll take a cruise. Those things are great. Everyone takes care of you. All you really have to do is look at the world through binoculars and think. Or not think. Rest. Figure things out. *(She looks at the world through binoculars for a moment.)* Alaska really is spectacular. Oh, look, a whale! *(She continues to look. After a moment.)* Yeah, going to Alaska was a great idea. There's just one thing I forgot. Dinner

(LEONARD and JUNETTE enter, dressed for dinner.)

LEONARD. Leonard Larson, from Minnesota. And this is my wife, Junette. It looks like we're at the same table!

JUNETTE. We'll be eating together all week!

EMMA. It turns out that Leonard's wife has an identical twin sister named June. June was born first, which is why Junette is named Junette.

JUNETTE. *(Bright)* It's true!

EMMA. You can't make this stuff up.

JUNETTE. So did you see that glacier today? My goodness.

LEONARD. Just great.

JUNETTE. And tomorrow, I guess we're gonna stop in Valdez.

LEONARD. See the pipeline. I been looking forward to that, let me tell you.

JUNETTE. Oh, I don't know ...

LEONARD. What?

JUNETTE. That pipeline tour. I just don't know.

LEONARD. *(Disappointed)* Well, we don't have to. I just thought ...

JUNETTE. I don't know.
LEONARD. I was kinda looking forward to it.
JUNETTE. Well.
LEONARD. We don't have to.
EMMA. Instead of seeing the pipeline, Leonard and Junette take a bus tour of the Worthington Glacier Mountain Pass, which carries you through Keystone Canyon, past Bridalveil Falls, three thousand feet up the side of a mountain. There, Leonard, who has a heart condition, goes into arrest.
JUNETTE. It was pretty scary, let me tell you!
LEONARD. It's nothing!
EMMA. He doesn't survive the night.
LEONARD. *(Bright)* I guess we should've gone to see the pipeline! *(Less bright)* I woulda liked to see that.
EMMA. Junette, I'm sorry.
JUNETTE. *(A little confused)* Oh, well, those things happen. Nice meeting you, Cathy.

(She and LEONARD go.)

EMMA. All told, I learn nothing in my cruise, except that Alaska is very far away, and the human race is at best a touching disappointment.

(The scene changes. TOMMY enters. He and EMMA meet in a restaurant.)

TOMMY. Hey, how's it going?
EMMA. Fine Just got back from Alaska.
TOMMY. Yeah, I heard. Must've been fantastic.
EMMA. It was very beautiful.

TOMMY. I bet. How was the cruise?
EMMA. Lotta food. Gained a few pounds.
TOMMY. I've heard that about those things.
EMMA. The Love Boat, with lots of old white people. Dutch crew, Nigerian porters. It was an exercise in imperialism with bad night club shows and bingo. They actually had sit-down aerobics.
TOMMY. *(Laughing)* Oh, no.

(Long pause.)

EMMA & TOMMY. So –

(They laugh.)

EMMA. Go ahead.
TOMMY. No, you.
EMMA. I was just going to say ... that, I did a lot of thinking while I was up there at the ends of the earth, and I got kind of lonely, frankly, and I don't want to lose you. *(Beat)* There was this old couple on the boat – ship, I mean, the ship – and at first I found them truly annoying, they were from "Minnesota", but they were also so *together*, you know, and then they lost each other, over a mistake, a foolish mistake, and I don't want that to happen to us. I mean, I don't really know what that whole thing in the restaurant was, but it was just a moment, a foolish mistake, and it doesn't matter as long as you and I are okay, because you are so dear to me, Tommy –
TOMMY. Emma. *(Beat)* Um.
EMMA. What?

TOMMY. This is awkward. *(Beat)* You should have let me go first.

EMMA. *(Beat)* Why?

TOMMY. Arthur feels that you have been a destructive influence. He, things aren't going as well on the fundraising, as he had hoped, the primary is right around the corner and he's very frustrated. He needs an outlet to express that frustration, and you seem to be providing that outlet.

EMMA. I wasn't talking about Arthur.

TOMMY. Yes you were.

EMMA. No, I wasn't. *(Beat)* Why are you?

TOMMY. Well. I am his campaign manager.

EMMA. And what am I?

TOMMY. You? You're nobody. *(Beat)* You should have apologized, Em.

EMMA. I didn't do anything. I didn't have anything to apologize for.

TOMMY. Yeah, well, I'm the guy's campaign manager. You can't expect me to side against him.

EMMA. *(Getting mad)* Side against Arthur, what does that mean?

TOMMY. Emma, come on. You're putting me in an awkward position. You have to at least acknowledge that.

EMMA. No, actually, I don't think I do.

TOMMY. Emma.

EMMA. What? I mean, what are you telling me, that you're cutting me off because Arthur's gone paranoid, that it wasn't enough for him to insult me in a restaurant, now he's got to take away my friends, too?

TOMMY. Look —

EMMA. No, you look! This is ridiculous! Tommy, are

VIEW OF THE DOME

you really willing to throw me away over nothing? Can you really just throw people away like that?

TOMMY. I'm sorry. I said what I have to say. I have to go.

(He starts to go.)

EMMA. Don't you dare walk away from me. I got you this job! No one would hire you! You were a huge drunk, and no one would even talk to you! I practically saved your life! *(He gives her a look.)* Well, it's true.

TOMMY. I had some problems. I've worked them out. I hope I haven't disappointed you or Arthur.

EMMA. *(Apologizing)* No, of course not. You've ... you seem to be doing a great job. How would I know? I don't know. Because no one will talk to me, because now, I'm nobody. *(Beat)* I just want this all to go away. I want it to have never happened. I don't understand it.

TOMMY. Why don't you just let go of this?

EMMA. I've been trying to.

TOMMY. No. You haven't.

EMMA. There's something I have to talk to you about, Tommy –

TOMMY. I am not talking to you anymore! *(Beat)* Look. I'm not trying to be mean, but you know – there's no big mystery here. You act like what's happened to you was crazy; well it wasn't. People just love to create a pecking order. It's everybody's favorite pastime, deciding who is more important than whom. This is why communism never worked. Oh, we're all equal. Yeah, right. It doesn't even work that way biologically. It doesn't work for monkeys, why should it work for us? You just ended up on the bad end of it for once. To Arthur, you were the least dangerous. The most expendable. It made him feel better to insult you so he did it.

EMMA. *(Cold)* What happened to Mr. Smith Goes to Washington? Democracy? A Man of the People?

TOMMY. He's still that. On a profound level, he has not compromised his ideals. I mean, this is just politics. And I have to go.

(He stands.)

    EMMA. Fuck you.
    TOMMY. Fine. I did my best.
    EMMA. Your best isn't very good. You're weak.

(He looks at her, doesn't answer, and goes. EMMA sits alone.)

EMMA. I mean, you think you have something to say, and then you find out that you don't because no one's listening. Is that possible? Like a tree falling in the forest, thoughts and feelings directed at no one don't exist? This is starting to BOTHER ME. ARTHUR!

(She turns, mid-roar, to find ARTHUR and ANNABETH in a big indiscreet clinch. For a moment, she doesn't put it together.)

EMMA. Oh, I'm sorry, I was looking for –

(ANNABETH and ARTHUR shriek and pull apart, guiltily shoving their clothes together.)

ARTHUR. This isn't what it looks like. We are both consenting adults, my marriage has been in trouble for many years –

ANNABETH. Arthur. Arthur! It's Emma, Arthur.

EMMA. Hi.

ARTHUR. Oh, my god.

EMMA. What are you doing, Arthur?

ARTHUR. How did you get in here?

EMMA. The kid at the desk said you were free. He said go on in –

ARTHUR. *(To ANNABETH)* He's fired.

ANNABETH. I'm on it.

EMMA. Oh, Arthur. Annabeth? Oh, ick. Oh.

ARTHUR. And get her out of here.

ANNABETH. Gladly.

EMMA. I'm not going anywhere!

ARTHUR. I'm calling security.

EMMA. Fine, call security. I'd love a scene. So would the press, I'm sure!

(Pause)

ANNABETH. Just hold off for a second, Arthur. I'm sure that won't be necessary. What do you want, Emma?

EMMA. *(Beat)* I want my money back.

ARTHUR. What?

EMMA. I gave you five thousand dollars for your campaign because I thought you were something that it turns out you're really not. I want my money back.

ARTHUR. *(To ANNABETH)* She's insane.

ANNABETH. Arthur, could you go into the next room

please? I'll handle this. Just wash your face, we have to be at the Rotary Club in fifteen minutes. *(Firm)* Arthur. I'm handling this.

(ARTHUR goes. ANNABETH considers EMMA.)

EMMA. Wow. He walks, he talks, and you can't see the wires.

ANNABETH. Emma, you're sounding like a bad soap opera. What you're doing here, I don't know, but I find it tacky.

EMMA. *I'm* tacky?

ANNABETH. You're embarrassing yourself. Your obsession with Arthur is abnormal. He told me you were in love with him. I didn't believe him. But this? Clearly, he was not imagining things. I'd think about that before I started babbling nasty little rumors to the press. Your motives aren't exactly pristine.

EMMA. My motives are fine. I'm not in love with Arthur. I'm mad at him because he squashed my ideals.

ANNABETH. *(Laughing a little)* What?

EMMA. Oh, never mind.

(Mouths: Why do I even bother?)

ANNABETH. You know, just for the record, I wanted you back. Geof Maddox was really taken with you and that sort of thing works with him. If you actually cared about Arthur, that might have occurred to you.

EMMA. What are you saying?

ANNABETH. I'm saying if you wanted to help, you had

your chance. All this talk about broken ideals. This is nobody's fault but your own.

EMMA. I can't follow this. Just give me my money, and I'll go.

ANNABETH. That is not going to happen.

ARTHUR. Give her the money.

(ARTHUR stands in the doorway.)

ANNABETH. I don't think that's wise, Arthur.

ARTHUR. If it will get her out of here, give her the money.

(ANNABETH shrugs, reaches into her jacket and pulls out a checkbook. She writes a check and hands it to EMMA.)

ANNABETH. Don't come back, Emma. It's embarrassing.

(She goes. EMMA looks at the check, at the audience as ARTHUR brings the podium downstage. EMMA listens.)

ARTHUR. Without question, America has fallen into a crisis of imagination. This great, troubled country, still the strongest force for freedom on this earth, seems to be slipping from our grasp. The two-party system has collapsed upon itself, imploding every issue into a middling sameness. Our leaders have shrunk into mere politicians, squabbling endlessly over nothing. And the most powerful voice now heard in our land is the shrill shriek of the hate-mongerer, claiming our airwaves, our heartland, claiming the highest legislative body of our nation. But we can tolerate this crippling cynicism no longer. We must build a bridge from our past to our future, and embrace the spirit of those democratic ideals, our own, which for the past two hundred years have provided a beacon for our suffering planet. "We hold these truths to be self-evident: that all men are created equal, that they are endowed by their Creator with certain inalienable rights, that among these are Life, Liberty and the Pursuit of Happiness." There is no quibbling here. There is only vision. Hope. The conviction that the human spirit can and will transcend its own pettiness. Only that conviction will save us now.

EMMA. I keep going back over that night. What I could have done to stop it.

(The restaurant comes together around her again. The others take their places as she speaks.)

ANNABETH. Now, how do you want to do the seating, Arthur? Four and one?

(EMMA looks over as ARTHUR considers this.)

ARTHUR. *(Quickly)* Oh, yes. That's exactly right. Four and one.
ANNABETH. David –

(She waves the waiter on.)

EMMA. And it always seems inexorable, in an odd way.
ANNABETH. We'll need a table for four, and a table for one.

VIEW OF THE DOME

DAVID. Right this way.

EMMA. The whole thing was so smooth. Like they'd practiced it.

TOMMY. Wait a minute. There are going to be five of us, aren't there? When the senator gets here –

EMMA. *(To TOMMY)* Apparently Annabeth and Arthur would prefer that I ate at a separate table.

ANNABETH. We'll set you up at the best single they have. David, can we get her the view of the capital dome?

DAVID. Anything for you, Annabeth.

EMMA. Like a secret handshake.

ARTHUR. Emma, you understand. This is strictly business.

DAVID. It's a little close to the kitchen and there is a draft ...

EMMA. And the only reason it was even this gracious was because graciousness is our excuse.

ANNABETH. Now, you and Tommy need to fill me in on your campaign strategy before the senator gets here.

EMMA. I'm just lucky we don't live in Rwanda.

ANNABETH. Arthur, this is awkward. Should I shoot her?

ARTHUR. Oh, yes. That's exactly right. Go ahead and shoot her.

(ANNABETH draws a gun and shoots EMMA, who goes down. ANNABETH then turns and pockets it.)

TOMMY & ARTHUR. Good shot! Good shot, Gilkey!
EMMA. I'm lucky this isn't the Vatican.
TOMMY. Arturo, why are these women talking?

ARTHUR. Good point. Guards! ANNO. DOMINI PATRI CHRISTO. NINA, PINTA, SANTA MARIA. AMEN.

(The waiter grabs EMMA; TOMMY grabs ANNABETH; they force them down as ARTHUR dismisses them with a cross.)

EMMA. I'm lucky this is America. Where democracy is a goal to which we, and our leaders, aspire.
ANNABETH. Now, how do you want to do the seating, Arthur? Four and one?

(EMMA looks over as ARTHUR considers this.)

ARTHUR. *(Quickly)* Oh, yes. That's exactly right. Four and one.
ANNABETH. David – *(She waves the waiter on.)* We'll need a table for four, and a table for one.
DAVID. Right this way.

(The waiter starts to move a place setting to the separate table.)

EMMA. So why should I go along with this nonsense?
TOMMY. There are going to be five of us, aren't there?
EMMA. I mean, if they want to play this game, I can play too, right?
ARTHUR. Emma, you understand.
EMMA. No, I don't, actually. I'm sitting here.

(She sits at the table. They all stare at her.)

VIEW OF THE DOME

ANNABETH. *(Horrified)* What is she doing?
EMMA. You invited me to dinner.
TOMMY. What are you *doing*?
ARTHUR. WHAT ARE YOU DOING?
EMMA. I want to meet the senator.

(They all scream. ARTHUR has a heart attack. EMMA leaps up from the table. ANNABETH goes to ARTHUR's dead body. She glares at EMMA.)

ANNABETH. He's dead. You killed him.
DAVID & TOMMY. MURDERER!
SENATOR. ASSASSIN!
EMMA. I'm sorry.
ARTHUR. You are an embarrassment.
EMMA. I'm sorry.
TOMMY. You're nobody.
EMMA. But, I drove.
ANNABETH. David, can we get her the view of the capital dome?
DAVID. Anything for you, Annabeth.
EMMA. Because finally there was nothing to be done.
DAVID. Anything for you, Annabeth.
EMMA. Somehow, it was a moment that would not be denied.
DAVID. Anything for you, Annabeth.
ARTHUR. *(Again speaking)* We must reclaim that idealistic heritage which was, at one time, our birthright. With the courage of our forebears we will reshape ourselves as a country and people of discipline, wisdom and compassion.

(Loud cheers and applause, as if at a convention. ARTHUR acknowledges.)

EMMA. I know it's vague, I know it's just rhetoric. But this is my problem. When people say things like that, I believe them. Or, I used to.

(The GOVERNOR enters. The others exit as they take a seat in a restaurant.)

GOVERNOR. Emma!
EMMA. Hello Governor!
GOVERNOR. Emma, I warned you.
EMMA. Oh, come on.
GOVERNOR. I mean it!
EMMA. I am not calling you "Uncle Jack." Everyone will think you're my sugar daddy.
GOVERNOR. If that's the way you feel about it ...

(He turns to go.)

EMMA. *(Protesting)* Uncle Jack ...
GOVERNOR. *(Sitting)* Much better. How's your dad?
EMMA. Oh, you know. The same. Lots of gardening, golfing, fighting with mom.
GOVERNOR. Your mother is a saint.
EMMA. She knows.
GOVERNOR. And your friend Arthur won the primary. This must be a very exciting time for you.
EMMA. Actually, I'm not involved in his campaign anymore.

GOVERNOR. No? You were so high on him.
EMMA. I found some things out. It's complicated.

(The waiter brings tea. She sips it.)

GOVERNOR. *(Worried)* Oh?
EMMA. I just had to put some distance there. It's nothing.
GOVERNOR. If it's nothing, then why don't you tell me?
EMMA. Because you're the governor.
GOVERNOR. It's sounding more and more like something you should tell the governor.
EMMA. I don't want to get anybody in trouble.
GOVERNOR. Emma, you introduced me to this man. I endorsed him. If there's something there that could come back and bite me, I need to know about it.
EMMA. No. There's nothing. Really. *(The GOVERNOR thinks about this, seems satisfied and goes for his tea.)* Just a little bit of erratic behavior. I'm sure it's nothing that you need to worry about.
GOVERNOR. What kind of erratic behavior?
EMMA. I don't want to damage Arthur! But the stress of the campaign seems to be making him increasingly unstable. He kind of lashed out at me at dinner, recently. It was very humiliating. And then when I tried to patch things up, he just became enraged. It got worse and worse until finally I just had to disengage myself from the whole thing.
GOVERNOR. Well, what set him off?
EMMA. Honestly, Uncle Jack, I don't know. Nothing, as far as I can tell. It was actually kind of psychotic. I mean, not

psychotic. Psychotic is too strong. I'm sure it's just stress! But maybe you should keep an eye out. Just in case it happens again with, you know. Someone important, God forbid.

GOVERNOR. You're important, Emma.

EMMA. Thanks, Uncle Jack. Do we have to talk about this? I hardly ever get to see you. Let's talk about something else.

GOVERNOR. *(Paternal)* Of course. Let me just make a phone call.

(He goes. EMMA watches, then sips her tea. Beat.)

EMMA. *(Musing)* Wow. That was easy. I didn't even have to lie.

SENATOR. Emma? *(The SENATOR approaches, delighted.)* Well, this is a pleasure. I haven't seen you since ...

EMMA. That fundraiser.

SENATOR. With your friend, Arthur. I see he's doing well in the polls.

EMMA. Actually, I think he's slipping.

SENATOR. Surely not. Annabeth tells me he's a huge hit.

EMMA. You don't think his rhetoric is sounding a little empty these days?

SENATOR. Well, whose isn't?

(He laughs. She laughs with him.)

EMMA. So true. They're throwing that big lunch for him today. You're probably on your way in, huh.

SENATOR. As a matter of fact, I am. Are you at my table?

EMMA. That would be novel, wouldn't it? Actually, I was going to skip it.

SENATOR. *(Disappointed)* Oh.

EMMA. Well, you don't have to go, do you? As I recall, you hate these things.

SENATOR. Annabeth has me down for the keynote address.

EMMA. Cause I was hoping we could sneak off. Go get some seafood or something.

SENATOR. *(Suggestive)* Lobster bisque?

EMMA. Lobster bisque.

SENATOR. Tuna tartare?

EMMA. Tuna tartare.

SENATOR. Creme brulee?

EMMA. Senator!

SENATOR. You're right, it's too risky. Well.

(He starts to go.)

EMMA. Then again, I've always liked creme brulee.

SENATOR. Emma. You're not talking about lunch.

EMMA. I'm not?

SENATOR. You're talking about politics.

EMMA. I'm very interested in politics.

(Listening intently, she steers him to the other side of the stage.)

SENATOR. It is a fascinating subject. You want to know what my life is like?

EMMA. Yes, I do.

SENATOR. I'm a prominent man. People are out to get me.

EMMA. It's so unfair, the system these days.

SENATOR. My home life is a mess. I never see my family.

EMMA. That's awful.

SENATOR. I don't make a lot of money. I go to battle every day up there on the hill, my work is murderously dull and the electorate I serve hates me. Why would anyone live this life?

(He casually drapes his arm around her. She sees where this is going but doesn't want to stop it.)

EMMA. Service?

SENATOR. Power! When I walk into a room, people applaud. My picture is in the newspapers, which quote the things I say. I eat delicious food. And women want me. Why should I give that up? It's the only reward I get. *(He is undressing her.)* Without the danger, I'm a petty bureaucrat. With it, I'm a senator!

(They fall into bed. Across the stage, ANNABETH, TOMMY and ARTHUR look about.)
(TOMMY, ANNABETH and ARTHUR enter. TOMMY is on cellphone.)

TOMMY. We can't find the senator.

ARTHUR. *(Panicking)* What do you mean, you can't find him? He's giving the keynote speech!

ANNABETH. *(Overlap)* Goddammit!

VIEW OF THE DOME   43

TOMMY. *(Reporting from phone)* He's not backstage. He's not on the floor.

ARTHUR. Annabeth, you take care of this.

TOMMY. He's not picking up his cellphone.

ANNABETH. I hate it when he does this!

ARTHUR. You said put yourself in my hands! You said I'll take care of everything!

TOMMY. *(Reporting)* There's a chance he's still in subcommittee –

ANNABETH. Get real. He's off screwing some campaign worker. The man is positively led around by his dick. Arthur, get Leon Panetta. He's always available. Tommy, call Jimmy Carville, he owes me bigtime. I'll see if John John is back from his honeymoon, yet.

(They go.)

EMMA. Make no mistake, the senator and I had a wonderful time. I needed it. It made me feel better. And there was an element of poetic justice that frankly added a certain zing to it all. Hey!

(The half-naked SENATOR takes her picture with a Polaroid camera. They playfully fight over it and take pictures of each other. They romp.)

SENATOR. I want to be able to see you whenever I want.

EMMA. In subcommittee hearings? I always wanted to be in politics.

(She snaps a picture of him.)

SENATOR. Just be careful who you show that to. Emma ...

(She keeps snapping pictures as he stands.)

EMMA. You look delicious ...

(He checks his watch.)

SENATOR. Oh my God. Look at the time. I gotta get to that dinner.

(The mood changes immediately. EMMA watches him dress.)

EMMA. What dinner? The one for Arthur?
SENATOR. *(Beat)* Yeah.
EMMA. I thought you weren't going to that.
SENATOR. Annabeth gave me such a hard time. I've missed the last three because of you, young lady. I can't skip another one.
EMMA. Did you tell her about us?
SENATOR. No. She may have guessed, though. Did you two have a fight or something?
EMMA. What makes you say that?
SENATOR. Just a vibe I get.
EMMA. Don't go. Come on, don't go. Please?
SENATOR. Emma. I have to.
EMMA. Because Annabeth says so.
SENATOR. Emma. Don't be a child.
EMMA. Don't treat me like one.
SENATOR. Oh, brother.

VIEW OF THE DOME

EMMA. What does she have on you?

SENATOR. Nothing.

EMMA. If she told you to dump me, would you?

SENATOR. You and I are having a wonderful time, Emma. Don't get like this.

EMMA. What would you do if she told you to dump me?

SENATOR. You're being ridiculous.

EMMA. Answer the question.

SENATOR. *(Point blank)* I'd want to know her reasons. And if they were good, I'd follow her advice. But it's not going to come to that, okay?

EMMA. No, not okay. For almost six weeks now, you and I –

SENATOR. Wait a minute. There's no "you and I here." What is – I knew this was going to happen. You girls, you always think you have rights. Well, you don't, okay? I'm a public figure, for god's sake. You know what you're doing? You're trying to control policy. You think you have the right to do that just because you're a good lay?

EMMA. I'm a what?

SENATOR. Look. You started this.

EMMA. That's not precisely how it happened.

SENATOR. Well, Annabeth never did this. She understands, this is business.

EMMA. And what business is that?

SENATOR. *(Beat)* You shouldn't have pushed.

(He grabs the photos and splits. She takes this in for a moment.)

EMMA. I do think there are moments in life when you

realize that everything you thought about yourself and the world were just never true. And that knowledge brings with it, frankly, great temptation.

(She reaches into a pocket and pulls out one last Polaroid. An anchorman appears in a spotlight.)

ANCHORMAN. And the hotly-contested race for Maryland's second district just got hotter. In an already scandal-ridden electoral season, a new star has appeared on the horizon as a young campaign worker has stepped forward to accuse congressional candidate Arthur Woolf and his sponsor, Senator Geoffrey Maddox of some rather exceptional forms of sexual misconduct. On the basis of rumor and innuendo alone, the polls are already fluctuating wildly. And while few facts are as yet available, pundits are leaping to comparisons with Donna Rice, Paula Jones, Jennifer Flowers, Fannie Fox, Kristine Keeler, Camila Parker Bowles, Lucy Mercer, Jessica Hahn, Rita Jenrette, every woman who's ever *met* Bob Packwood, Judith Exner, Kim Novak, Sherry Rowlands, and Marilyn Monroe. We take you live to Baltimore, Maryland.

(EMMA turns and speaks. Flashbulbs pop.)

EMMA. Three months ago, I accompanied the candidate and his campaign manager to a dinner and a fundraiser. At the time, I was not an important part of the campaign – they even sat me at a different table in the restaurant – but as soon as the senator showed interest in me, things changed. Arthur made it clear that I should be ... "nice" to the senator. He really needed his endorsement, so I was basically told to do whatever had to be done. If I cooperated, he said, I would be rewarded.

ANCHORMAN. And you took that to mean sexual favors?

EMMA. That is what it meant, yes.

ANCHORMAN. And were you compensated for these favors?

EMMA. Only recently. The senator and I met for for the last time a week ago, and I told him I was pregnant. At that time, he decided he wanted nothing more to do with me. When I told Arthur, he gave me a check for $5000 and told me to get an abortion. I realized then that I could no longer participate in their sick, twisted morality.

ANCHORMAN. You realize that both the candidate and the senator have denied your allegations.

EMMA. Well, that doesn't surprise me. They're both pretty heavily into denial. Anyway, I have the check, and some pictures of myself with the senator. *(She shows these things to the ANCHORMAN.)* Oh. And here's my doctor's report. I'm just starting my second trimester.

(She shows it to the ANCHORMAN.)

ANCHORMAN. *(Clears his throat, to audience.)* As I said, the offices of both the candidate and the senator have issued denials at this time. However, several supporters of opposing candidate Oliver Riley have hailed this young woman as a heroine and a prophet for the new morality. They are calling for a senate investigation into this matter.

(He nods, and exits. EMMA looks at the audience.)

EMMA. This town is about spin. They spun the story one way, I spun it another. Oh. Did I tell you I was pregnant?

(Flashbulbs pop. A crowd of reporters descend.)

REPORTER #1. Emma –
REPORTER #2. Over here, Emma –
REPORTER #3. Emma, could we have a statement?
EMMA. I made a mistake. I didn't stand up for myself. I'm doing that now.
REPORTER #1. Is there anything you want to say to Senator Maddox?
EMMA. I'm sorry he's going to be hurt by this, but frankly he should've kept it in his pants.

(They laugh.)

REPORTER #2. And, why have you decided to come forward with this story now? By your own admission, you were quite happy with this arrangement for months. What made you change your mind?
EMMA. I just realized that men who could behave like this had no business serving in the highest legislative body of our land. I mean, I talk to people, and there's this sense that we can do better, we can be a better people, but we need leaders who will understand our hunger of spirit. Our yearning. Our hope that humanity is not merely degraded.
REPORTER #3. We're living in the gutter but looking at the stars, huh?
REPORTERS #1, 2 & 3. Yeah, yeah, yeah, yeah.

(They go.)

EMMA. I can't believe it took me so long to figure this out. When you're good, everybody stomps on you. When you're bad, you end up in the newspaper. I'm going to be in the newspaper!

RICHARD. Can I speak with you?

(EMMA looks over. RICHARD, a carefully dressed party organizer smiles at her politely.)

EMMA. Actually, I'm kind of tired. The press conference went longer than I thought.

RICHARD. Yes, I saw. I'm Richard Riley. People in my organization were impressed with what you did. You're a brave woman.

EMMA. Thank you.

RICHARD. Well, I'm afraid what you're doing is going to lead you into a lot of very difficult, very frightening situations. You are aware of that, aren't you?

EMMA. Actually, I hadn't really thought about what happens next —

RICHARD. Of course not. You were just trying to do what was right. Let the world know who these men are.

EMMA. Yes.

RICHARD. Unfortunately, Washington is not a town that respects someone with a really pure motive. People here don't seem to understand that once in a while, maybe someone just wants to do what's right.

EMMA. No. They don't.

RICHARD. Why don't you let us help you?

EMMA. Well – who are you?

RICHARD. We are the Keepers of the American Promise.

(BELLA and AUGUST enter, bustling about EMMA, making her comfortable.)

BELLA. She's pregnant, Richard! Would you offer her a seat?

(AUGUST gives her a chair.)

AUGUST. Congratulations. I know that might be hard for you to hear, under these circumstances –
EMMA. Well –
BELLA. But babies are great. You're going to have a great time.
EMMA. I hope so. I'm a little –
AUGUST. We think you're very brave.
BELLA. Very.
AUGUST. Aren't politicians awful?
BELLA. Just terrible. What they did to you.
EMMA. It was pretty –
AUGUST. It's certainly time for a change. Washington just doesn't understand what people want any more.
BELLA. What *good* people want.
EMMA. Who are you again?
BELLA. Emma. Some of the fine points of our philosophies are not going to match up. But we want you to know that you are not alone. The system doesn't work anymore. A lot of people realize that. And we're trying to organize, on a grassroots level, to rebuild the country from the bottom up. Our schools. Our cities. Our communities. These are the things we're concerned about. I think that's what you're concerned about, too.

VIEW OF THE DOME 51

RICHARD. Besides, they fucked you over. Forgive me, for such language, but they did.

AUGUST. Richard, I really think –

RICHARD. Look. Unless we spell things out, they're going to crucify her. Emma. This is the hill. No one gives a shit about women here. And no one cares about the truth. Remember Tailhook? Remember Anita Hill? That's what's going to happen to you. You are about to become the biggest lesbian fantasizing lovesick crazy bitch the world has ever seen. Unless you let us help you.

EMMA. Help me how?

(LANCE, a flaming costume designer, approaches, carrying sweaters and skirts.)

LANCE. God, no. Absolutely not. Everything has to go. SHEILA! I'm going to need the rack of Laura Ashley. *(Fingering EMMA's jacket)* Oh, this is *fa*bulous. Rayon and wool, right? These new blends are unbe*lie*vable. What size are you? Six? And you can eat anything, right? I hate you, I really do.

(He holds up a hideous pink sweater.)

EMMA. I'm not wearing this.

LANCE. Sweetheart, you can't go out there as a fallen woman, it's completely unsympathetic. Even Ingrid Bergman couldn't pull it off. *Notorious*?

EMMA. That's my favorite movie!

LANCE. *(Impersonating Ingrid Bergman)* Why won't you believe me, Dev? Just a little bit.

LANCE & EMMA. Oh, Dev! Dev! Dev!

LANCE. She's fabulous, of course, but people just didn't want to see it. And with all due respect, dear, your story is wretched enough. You don't want to look the part. We have to go much more Midwest ...

EMMA. Nobody wear this stuff. Even in the Midwest.

LANCE. I wouldn't lie about clothes this ugly. Isn't this hideous? I love it! SHEILA!

(SHEILA enters, pushing a rack of Laura Ashley dresses as LANCE continues to dress a resisting EMMA.)

SHEILA. *(Frazzled)* I don't know, Lance. This is all I could find and I was sure we had just a mess of them from that Junior League tag sale ...

LANCE. Those whores. They promised me a lot of at least twenty. Oh, this is just pathetic ...

EMMA. I'm not wearing this!

SHEILA. That's not my battle, honey. You and I are gonna accessorize. Some pretty earrings. A little something at the neck. I love your hair. Is that your real color? Wait a minute, what happened to that little gold rosary?

EMMA. I don't know ...

SHEILA. I'm telling you, this stuff will make all the difference. Cause when you look good, you feel good. And when you feel good, you do good. That's what I say. It's not strictly true, but what the hell.

(She drapes it on her arm as RICHARD enters, businesslike, and oversees the final touches.)

RICHARD. Here's the new statement. The rosary's too much.

SHEILA. I like it ...

RICHARD. It's too Catholic. We need a broader appeal.

(SHEILA goes after her with a hairbrush. RICHARD hands EMMA some pages.)

EMMA. I can't say this. These people used to be friends of mine.

RICHARD. Wait until you hear what they say about you.

(ANNABETH, ARTHUR and TOMMY enter as the others leave.)

ANNABETH. That fucking *cunt.*

TOMMY. Has anyone tried to talk to her? I mean, maybe if we just tried to have one conversation. She can't be completely crazy –

ANNABETH. Have you read the newspapers?

TOMMY. I'm just saying –

ANNABETH. Fuck her, I'm not talking to that bitch. I'm taking out a fucking contract on her life. I told you, Arthur, I told you not to give her the money –

ARTHUR. If you didn't want to give it to her, you shouldn't have given it to her! You were the one who made out the check!

ANNABETH. Only because you told me to!

ARTHUR. I said, call security! I said, she's insane!

ANNABETH. That's my point! How the hell did you ever let her into this fucking campaign?

TOMMY. Things were fine when she was involved. The whole mistake was kicking her out in the first place –

ANNABETH. I'm sunk. I'm fucking dead meat in this town. Geoffrey Maddox won't return my fucking phone calls, did you know that? Has anyone thought about that? You introduced her to a major fucking senator and she fucked us both, Arthur, that's not the sort of thing people forget around here –

ARTHUR. You take care of this, Annabeth. You said, put yourself in my hands, I'll take care of everything –

ANNABETH. I swear, if it was legal I'd take out a fucking contract on her life. I'd rip that baby out of her womb with my bare hands if the press wouldn't be so shitty about it.

TOMMY. You think she's really pregnant, then?

ANNABETH. Of course she's fucking pregnant! It was the first thing I checked!

TOMMY. So, who's the father? I mean, we don't really think it's Senator Maddox, do we?

(Silence. ARTHUR and ANNABETH look at him, exhausted.)

ANNABETH. We don't know, Tommy. He won't return my phone calls. He has distanced himself from our campaign. *(Beat)* I'm fucking sunk in this town.

TOMMY. So what do we do?

ANNABETH. I'll spread some money around her firm, see who I can get to smear her.

TOMMY. You're not going to come up with anything.

ANNABETH. Don't be smug. There's always somebody who got passed over for a promotion, or got turned down for a date. Arthur, what about law school?

ARTHUR. What about it?

ANNABETH. She fuck any of her professors? Cheat on a test? Plagiarize anything?

ARTHUR. I'll come up with something.

ANNABETH. Tommy, you'll make the statement.

ARTHUR. *I'll* make the statement.

ANNABETH. Arthur, you have to stay above this.

ARTHUR. They're not above it.

ANNABETH. Of course they're not, they're *republicans*.

(RICHARD stands at a podium and reads a statement.)

RICHARD. We insist that this matter be given the fullest scrutiny.

(TOMMY approaches the other podium.)

TOMMY. This woman was only peripherally involved in Mr. Woolf's campaign, for a very short period of time.

RICHARD. This man was running a prostitution ring out of his campaign headquarters!

TOMMY. The candidate was aware that she had a history of mental illness dating back to when she was once a student in law school, but it was our understanding that those problems had been resolved.

RICHARD. If, as Mr. Woolf claims, this young woman is emotionally disturbed, that makes their behavior even more reprehensible!

TOMMY. We have documentation from several psychiatrists and ex-boyfriends. She is a nymphomaniac and a pathological liar.

RICHARD. We have also uncovered evidence that the campaign funds used to pay this woman off may have come from an illegal foreign bank account connected to several failed Savings and Loans. I wouldn't be surprised if this conspiracy reached all the way to the presidency.

TOMMY. Oh, for heaven's sake!

(The two men's arguments start to overlap.)

RICHARD. You are not going to sweep this under the rug. Your candidate and Senator Maddox were incapable of controlling their penises, well, you can just reap the rewards of that, because you're in the big leagues now, buster, and the rules of the game have been made pretty damn clear these past few years, so –

TOMMY. *(Overlap)* I'm sick to death of you and your little troop of fanatics, ranting on and on about what's right and true and godly when none of you give a shit about the truth, or god for that matter, all you care about is winning and you'll stoop to absolutely any kind of lie you Bible thumping CONTROL FREAK!

(RICHARD and TOMMY square off. EMMA enters, watching. EMMA carries a bowl of popcorn. She has been transformed into a modern-day virgin type.)

RICHARD. FORNICATOR!
TOMMY. HYPOCRITE!
RICHARD. HOMOSEXUAL!
TOMMY. NEO-NAZI!
RICHARD. LIBERAL!

VIEW OF THE DOME

TOMMY. Oh, fuck you, you fascist scum.
RICHARD. Yeah, fuck you, too.

(They reach across the divide and shake hands, congratulating each other as after a debate. RUSH LIMBAUGH comes on the television.)

RUSH. I'm sure I should be surprised, but I'm not. The new way to get elected, according to the democrats, is to pimp your campaign workers for political favors. Have you heard about this one? A candidate for congress told one of his campaign workers to sleep with a well-known senator in order to get an endorsement. And you thought you had seen it all. Not yet! Now, this woman is apparently some sort of ex-feminazi, and it's hard to have sympathy for her because out of party loyalty, I guess, she actually went along with this sick arrangement for at least three months. Yeah, she's a real prize. Scratch a feminist, find a prostitute. And it turns out she's pregnant! And I for one am not sanguine about her shall we say "maternal instincts," are you? The chances of this little tyke running afoul of the law are just a little too rich for my blood. More police, more court costs, more prisons — more of your tax dollars being spent to address the misdeeds of the liberal elite! Not to mention the cost to the victims of this whore's demon seed! It's a good thing we have the death penalty, that's all I have to say! I mean, if it were up to me, I'd say we should just drown the kid at birth!
EMMA. Oh, my God!
RUSH. Oh, what did you expect, a baby shower?

(He goes.)

LANCE. Doll, you do know how to stir things up.

EMMA. I just don't know about this. Why do I have to look like the Virgin Mary? Everybody knows I'm *not* the Virgin Mary.

LANCE. Hey, you're getting a little bit of a pooch here.

EMMA. I am not.

LANCE. Oh my god. Isn't that the most beautiful thing you've even seen? *(Calling off.)* Sheila get the baby clothes!

EMMA. *Baby* clothes. I'm only twenty weeks!

LANCE. Oh come on, aren't you getting excited? Little shoes and socks and those tiny baby overalls, hats, little tiny baseball caps –

EMMA. It is king of great. I felt the baby move the other day.

LANCE. Ohmygod. Can I?

(He holds his hand over her stomach.)

EMMA. Well, sure, but you probably won't feel anything. It doesn't happen all that ...

(He starts, holds up his hand. She falls silent as he feels the baby move.)

LANCE. Is that it?
EMMA. That's it.
LANCE. Just that little flutter?
EMMA. Wait a minute.

(They pause.)

VIEW OF THE DOME 59

LANCE. *(Laughing)* Isn't that something? *(They smile at each other.)* You're so lucky. I can't wait to have children.

EMMA. You want children?

LANCE. I love children. You should have seen me in my heyday. I was the baby-sitting queen of America.

EMMA. Really?

LANCE. Oh honey, I'm telling you, they were lining up around the block. My dance card was *full*. Some nights I had four or five of 'em in my mother's living room crawling all over me, crawling all over each other, diapers everywhere – I was in pig heaven.

EMMA. It sounds awful.

LANCE. I'll tell you this much, there's nothing better than putting a baby to sleep. Children are life's holy blessing.

EMMA. Yeah, it's what they grow into that worries me.

LANCE. I think I could be satisfied with maybe seven or eight. Course, I have to find the right woman first.

(He goes back to work. EMMA looks at him.)

EMMA. It must be hard.

LANCE. What's that?

EMMA. Well, you know. Being a gay man who wants kids.

LANCE. *(Beat)* What makes you say that?

EMMA. Well – I don't know. It's hard for gay men to have kids, isn't it? It just seems to me there'd be a lot to work out. Logistically.

LANCE. And what makes you think I'm a homosexual?

EMMA. *(Beat)* Well, gee, Lance, I mean – Oh. You're kidding, right?

LANCE. You think this is funny?

EMMA. Well – No. I'm sorry. Let's forget I said it.

LANCE. I don't want to forget it. What you've accused me of is very serious. I don't see how you can ask me to forget this!

EMMA. I'm not accusing you of anything! I just thought – I mean, come on, you're so – flaming. Lance –

LANCE. Homosexuality is a sin. It is s perversion of nature. The Bible is very clear about this.

EMMA. The Bible?

LANCE. You don't believe in the Bible?

EMMA. Well, I don't know. I mean, some of it seems okay, but –

LANCE. You can't pick and choose among the word of God, Emma. Do you know what you're saying?

EMMA. I didn't, I just – look. I don't think there's anything wrong with, you know. Being gay. So, I'm sorry. I misunderstood.

LANCE. Yes. You did.

EMMA. So I'm sorry.

(Beat)

LANCE. It's all right. But you should read your Bible. It – what you're talking about – is disgusting to God.

EMMA. I'm sorry to hear that.

LANCE. It's just that I've been accused of this before. This is why – for years people trusted me with their children, and I loved every one of them. You would've had to strike me dead before I let anyone hurt those children.

EMMA. I know that.

LANCE. Then someone decided it was unnatural. I was unnatural. I never had a girlfriend, it just didn't happen, all of a sudden, people started thinking – well, I don't have to tell you, you thought the same thing. And they decided their children were not safe. I just, I can't take this lightly, Emma.

EMMA. I'm sorry.

(LANCE exits.)

SHEILA. Emma! You're on in five minutes.

(EMMA turns, confused. The lights come on her.)

EMMA. Oh, I'm sorry – I'm just so confused about all this –

SHEILA. Honey, no. Confusion's bad. They'll just eat you up.

EMMA. Oh! I don't know.

SHEILA. Now, you can do this! I know you can! The world wants to hear from you. All those normal people out there, they're sick of these politicians. They want to hear someone real talk about the way things are. They want to hear the truth. Come on now. Tell us who you are.

EMMA. I'm a concerned citizen.

SHEILA. That's right.

EMMA. I am not insane.

SHEILA. We know you're not. Emma, just tell the truth.

(The SENATORS arrive.)

SENATOR A. You are not on trial here. This is a simple

investigatory hearing which should allow us to gather the facts.

SENATOR B. The senate is grateful to you for bringing these matters to our attention. And may I just take a minute to assure the public, I knew *nothing* about this prostitution ring. I was in no way involved.

(He laughs, uneasy. The other SENATORS look at him as they set up before her.)

SENATOR C. I'd like to begin by asking the witness to provide us with a short synopsis of events beginning I think with the evening you first met Senator Maddox. According to your statement here, the meeting took place in a restaurant here in Washington.

EMMA. Yes.

SENATOR C. *(Reading off his copy of her statement)* You came with the candidate and his party with the intention of meeting the Senator, but you ended up sitting at another table. Is that correct?

EMMA. Yes.

SENATOR C. Why was that?

EMMA. I never was entirely clear about that.

SENATOR A. You came together?

EMMA. Yes. I drove.

SENATOR A. You drove! And then the candidate, who I believe is a friend of yours –

EMMA. Was a friend of mine, yes.

SENATOR A. He asked you to sit at another table?

EMMA. Yes.

SENATOR B. Not very good manners.

(The SENATORS concur.)

SENATOR A. Not good manners? It was downright rude! Didn't that hurt your feelings?

EMMA. Yes, actually it did –

SENATOR A. I should think so! Did he ever apologize?

EMMA. No, in fact, he became angry with me.

SENATOR B. He became angry with you? Why?

EMMA. You know, I never could really figure that out, either.

SENATOR C. Now, wait a minute. I just want to make sure I've got this straight. He completely humiliates you by asking you to sit at another table, and then *he* gets mad at you.

SENATOR A. That takes some nerve! I mean, she *drove*.

SENATOR C. So what did you do?

EMMA. Well, then I tried to suggest we just put it behind us, but he was more and more angry –

SENATOR A. Unbelievable!

EMMA. It just seemed to keep going, no matter what I did –

SENATOR C. It became a point of pride? He decided he was too important to deal with it, and you got left in the dust?

EMMA. I guess.

SENATOR A. I hate it when men do that. You give them a little bit of power, and their manners go right out the window.

SENATOR B. But he wasn't even elected yet!

SENATOR A. Well, it's a good thing. Can you imagine how insufferable he'd be if he actually got in congress?

SENATOR B. Oh, my god.

SENATOR A. We've all missed a speeding bullet if you ask me.

EMMA. He's really not that bad.

SENATOR A. Oh, no. Don't defend him. There's no excuse for this kind of nonsense.

EMMA. But the guy he's running against is no saint, either.

SENATOR. C. Why? What did he do?

SENATOR A. Did he do this? *(He bonks SENATOR B on the head with a gavel. SENATOR C stands up and pulls his nose. For a brief, hysterical moment, they whack each other crazily and then sit down.)* Is that what he did? Because we won't stand for that!

SENATOR B. The idea!

SENATOR C. This is the senate! We insist that people BEHAVE! *(SENATOR A bonks him on the head. SENATOR C glares at him.)* Why, I oughta ...

(And they all go at each other again, in a fast, furious slapstick fight.)

EMMA. Hey! HEY! *(They all stop and stare at her.)* What are you doing?

SENATOR A. We were just making a point. If your friend wants to be in congress, that means you have to behave better, not worse, than everyone else.

SENATOR C. Well put.

SENATOR B. I couldn't agree more.

SENATOR C. I have everything I need.

SENATOR A. Same here.

SENATOR B. *(To EMMA)* Thank you for your time. The country needs people as civic minded as you are.

(They start to exit.)

EMMA. Wait a minute! I mean – don't you want to talk about this prostitution ring?

SENATOR C. What about it?

SENATOR B. I knew *nothing* about it. I just want to make sure everyone knows that.

EMMA. Well, of course you didn't, you moron, it didn't exist! I made it up!

(She stops herself. Pause.)

SENATOR C. What are you trying to tell us, Emma?

EMMA. All right, look. The men I was working for disappointed me greatly. I did feel the need to let people know, and this way a way I thought I could do it. I mean, if I just told my story, no one would care, petty acts of meanness and cruelty don't seem to make an impression on people anymore. To get anybody's attention, you need a big, vulgar scandal, even though, if you asked me, what actually happened was worse than this stupid story I made up. But no one would understand that, and I was angry, so ... I'm sorry. I never meant –

SENATOR C. No need to apologize.

SENATOR B. I couldn't agree more.

SENATOR C. I have everything I need.

SENATOR A. Same here.

SENATOR B. *(To EMMA)* Thank you for your time. The country needs people as civic minded as you are.

(They exit.)
(SHEILA enters.)

SHEILA. Emma! You're on in five minutes.

(EMMA turns, confused.)

EMMA. Oh, I'm sorry – I'm just so confused about all of this –
SHEILA. Now, what I'd tell you about confusion!
EMMA. Oh – I don't know ...
SHEILA. The world wants to hear from you! All those people out there! Someone real's gotta tell the truth! Normal people are sick of this shit! The truth will set you free! Hallelujah! Praise Jesus!

(She starts to sing in tongues.)

EMMA. Sheila?
SHEILA. *(Fast to switch back to reality)* Emma. Just tell the truth.

(She goes. EMMA looks at the audience.)

SENATOR C. *(Voice over)* WHY DON'T YOU TELL US WHAT HAPPENED THAT NIGHT?
EMMA. I was introduced to Senator Maddox. He seemed interested in me. It was suggested that I should be nice to him because it might help Arthur's campaign. *(Beat)* That is what I did.

(The lights change. The SENATORS leave. EMMA sits alone on stage. LANCE enters.)

LANCE. Hey. How you doing?

EMMA. Oh. Lance. Hi.

LANCE. I thought it went good. The hearing.

EMMA. Yeah, it went fine.

LANCE. I mean, you seemed a little nervous at first.

EMMA. Did I?

LANCE. But you looked fabulous.

EMMA. Thanks.

LANCE. Richard really thought it went well. And I thought – to tell you the truth, I think you're the bravest person I've ever met.

EMMA. Oh. No.

LANCE. To stand there and admit to the whole country what you've done wrong –

EMMA. Yeah, well –

LANCE. And then to do whatever you have to, to set it right, no matter what the cost –

EMMA. It's really not what you think, Lance.

LANCE. It's meant a lot to me. I've learned a lot from you. *(Pause. EMMA sighs.) (Continuing)* I'm sorry I took your head off the other day.

EMMA. It's okay. I shouldn't have said anything.

LANCE. No. You were right. *(Pause)* When you said, that you thought I was – that way. You were right.

EMMA. *(Beat)* I was?

LANCE. I've tried to fight it. I've prayed a lot. I see a counselor. But I just don't seem to be able to overcome it.

EMMA. Well, Lance, maybe that's because there's really nothing wrong with it. Have you thought about that?

LANCE. That's what the devil would like me to believe.

EMMA. Oh. The devil.

LANCE. Anyway. You don't need to hear about my

problems. I just wanted you to know. You were so brave about admitting your sins. I thought I should do the same.

EMMA. Lance, you're fine –

(RICHARD enters.)

RICHARD. You were wonderful, Emma! Your testimony means a great deal, not just to us, but to the entire country.

LANCE. I was just telling her.

RICHARD. Lance, do you think that tomorrow we could go for a slightly more sophisticated look? I think we've erred too much on the side of caution. She looked like a perverse school girl out there.

LANCE. Maybe a blazer –

RICHARD. And lose the head band. Emma, we've made some revisions in your testimony. We came up with some evidence that implicates the first lady, and it would be good if you could lay some groundwork for that.

(He hands her pages.)

EMMA. No, no, no. I'm not doing this anymore. This is bullshit. I'm not going back there. I'm not testifying any more.

RICHARD. I think you are. Lance, I'd like to speak with Emma alone, please.

LANCE. I'll be praying for you, Emma.

(LANCE exits.)

EMMA. You know, this whole thing is a lie. You know I made it up. Don't you?

RICHARD. Of course.

EMMA. And that doesn't matter to you.

RICHARD. Not one bit. Sit down, Emma.

EMMA. I'm not doing what you tell me anymore, Richard. You're a bunch of fucking hypocrites, couching all this bile and hate in terms of righteousness --

RICHARD. Now, I'm not going to have a conversation with you about hypocrisy, Emma. With all due respect, you could teach a class. I said, sit down. *(She does.)* I mean, what do you think this is? What do you think is going on here? Do you honestly think you can just do whatever you want and there will be no consequences? For god's sake, we could take your child from you. We could send you to jail. And if you cross me, we'll do it. Do you understand that?

EMMA. *(Beat)* You can't take my baby.

RICHARD. Well, it's wonderful to hear that that concerns you. I wasn't sure. So, you want this baby. You care about this baby.

EMMA. Yes.

RICHARD. Then you listen to me. You've perpetrated a fraud on the entire nation! You've tried to interfere with the workings of the senate! You're clearly mentally unstable. So if we want that kid, we're not going to have any trouble getting it. And then we're going to give it to some nice, Christian family to raise. Am I getting through to you? *(Pause)* Look. There's no need to throw threats at each other. You came here because you belonged here. You didn't like the way people were behaving, so you decided to punish them. No one held a gun to your head. You did it because it made sense to you. You're just like us. You understand righteousness, and anger, and retribution. You understand the human condition. So stop whining, and play by the rules. Don't ever talk back to me again.

(He goes. Beat)

EMMA. *(To audience)* All right. I admit it. I've made some mistakes. But, you know, I didn't start this. You saw what happened. You were with me every step of the way. And it all made sense to you, I mean, I didn't hear anyone trying to stop me, now did I? YOU'RE IN THIS EVERY BIT AS DEEP AS I AM. I'm sorry. Once again, it seems that I am in need of a little perspective. *(MARJORIE enters as the stage changes into a bar. A drunk sits at another table.) (To MARJORIE)* It was, somebody said this, I remember, but I can't remember who, said this thing about culture and objectivity, that when a culture values objectivity and, you know, *reason*, then that's good, because that means we're all in this together, we're trying to find this collective objective *thing*, right? But that doesn't always happen, sometimes whole cultures, whole, like, America, slide toward subjectivity, everything is me me me, and then, all hell breaks loose, no one is talking to each other anymore, it's like we've all got these reflector sunglasses on and the reflector part is on the inside, so we just keep looking at ourselves until we're completely blind and then there's nothing holding us together anymore, and I didn't mean to do it, but I got angry, and I thought anger was a good thing, because it helps you fight for change, but it's also dangerous because it's so sub*jec*tive, you think you're helping the world, and you're the problem!

That's just it, isn't it, the lesson is, there's nothing you can do. I'm sorry. I've just, I've done terrible things and I don't know how to set it right.

(She drinks. MARJORIE smiles at her, happy.)

MARJORIE. Hey, I saw you on TV today.
EMMA. What?
MARJORIE. I thought you looked great. That dress you had on was adorable. That's a good look for you. Kind of young.
EMMA. Marjorie –
MARJORIE. Oh, come on, cheer up! I mean, this is very exciting. They were talking about you on the news, too. And I was like, wow. I know her.
EMMA. What were they saying?
MARJORIE. Oh, you know. I don't know. But you should be having a great time. Everyone is paying all this attention to you. You get to meet all these famous people.
EMMA. I'm in the middle of a terrible scandal.
MARJORIE. Yeah, but you're on TV! I mean, this stuff doesn't happen everyday. I think you should enjoy it, is all I"m saying.
EMMA. Well, you're in a good mood.
MARJORIE. Oh, yeah. I feel great. I'm on prozac, did I tell you?
EMMA. No, actually, you didn't.
MARJORIE. Oh, yeah. I love it. You should try it. I mean, with all due respect, Emma, you're getting a little negative these days.
EMMA. I realize that. I was counting on you to be negative too. That's sort of why I called you.

MARJORIE. Well, yeah, but I'm on drugs now.
EMMA. So you said.
MARJORIE. OK. I love you.
EMMA. *(Sour)* I love you, too.

(MARJORIE goes. The drunk at the next table calls at her as she leaves.)

E.T. BLACK. Hey! Do you know who I am?
MARJORIE. Oh, of course! Hi! How's it going?
E.T. BLACK. You know me?
MARJORIE. Oh! No. I thought you were someone else. I'm sorry.

(She smiles and goes.)

E.T. BLACK. *(To his drink)* Well, fuck you, I don't know who you are, either.

(He drinks. After a pause, EMMA calls from her table.)

EMMA. Hey, E.T.
E.T. BLACK. What?
EMMA. I know who you are.
E.T. BLACK. You do?
EMMA. You're E.T. Black. You're a famous screenwriter.
E.T. BLACK. You know who I am? Wait a minute. You know who I am?

(The drunk stares at her, stands and slowly staggers over to her table.)

EMMA. Yeah, you're E.T. Black. I met you here a couple months ago.

E.T. BLACK. Fuck. Did I sleep with you?

EMMA. No.

E.T. BLACK. I can't remember anything anymore ... Wait a minute. I know who you are.

EMMA. Yeah, we met a couple months ago.

E.T. BLACK. You're the girl from the senate hearings. Not Anita Hill, the other one. With the weird story. I know all about you.

EMMA. *(Cold)* Good.

E.T. BLACK. Yeah, Hollywood is all over you. You got everything – sex, money, politics, a good part for a woman. They want me to write a movie about you.

EMMA. They do?

E.T. BLACK. Nobody's called you yet? Well, isn't that a fucking kick. They're pitching your story to me, and they don't even own the rights. Assholes. Listen, when they come after you, first thing they're gonna do is try and rob you blind. Don't be stupid. Hire a lawyer and hold out for seven figures.

EMMA. Thanks for the tip.

E.T. BLACK. Yeah, like you need to be warned about how the world works.

EMMA. And you'll write the screenplay?

E.T. BLACK. Oh, fuck, no. I passed. I'm not getting involved with this. I mean, with all due respect, sweetheart, that story you told is a complete whopper.

EMMA. *(Beat)* Is that so?

E.T. BLACK. Oh, come on. I may be a drunk, but I'm still a writer. I can tell when something's made up.

EMMA. I don't know what you're talking about.

E.T. BLACK. Yeah, of course you have to take that position. And most of them will fall for it. I said to these guys, these producers, she's *lying*, and they all stared at me like I was insane, of course, they all tell so many lies per second they can't tell the difference anymore, but what am I supposed to do? You can't fictionalize a piece of fiction, where would that fucking put you? You keep building on something fake and the next thing you know, you got just some psychic no man's land, the American government, or Hollywood, some weird fucking place where nothing has to make sense anymore, it just has to move or make money. Everyone keeps acting like two lies make a fucking truth, when that isn't exactly how it works, hasn't that *occurred* to anybody? How long do they expect me to go along with this? That's all I'm saying! I'm E.T. Black, I'm a *writer*, for God's sake, if this were the nineteenth century I'd be having lunch with *Disraeli* and these guys just keep paying me to lie, but there are limits, all right? There are fucking limits!

EMMA. You won't write my story.

E.T. BLACK. No I will not.

EMMA. Because you have too much integrity. Is that what you're saying?

E.T. BLACK. Sweetie, it shows up at the oddest times.

(He stands to go.)

EMMA. I just put a spin on things. Everybody does it.

E.T. BLACK. Yeah. That's the first one you tell yourself. You know – you're gonna have a kid. You should be thinking about these things.

EMMA. Oh, I am.

VIEW OF THE DOME

E.T. BLACK. And you shouldn't be drinking. It's not good for the baby.

DAVID. It's apple juice.

E.T. BLACK. Well, that's good. Don't start drinking, okay? It doesn't help. You think it does, but it doesn't.

EMMA. Thanks for the tip. *(He goes.) (To audience.)* So, it turns out I have less integrity than a Hollywood screenwriter.

DAVID. Hey, are you E.T. Black?

E.T. BLACK. You know I am. I drink in here all the time.

DAVID. I love your work, man.

E.T. BLACK. You're just saying that.

DAVID. No, I'm not. You're the best writer in America.

E.T. BLACK. Really?

DAVID. Ever since you started drinking in here, I went out and rented all your movies. You're a fucking genius, man.

E.T. BLACK. You watched my movies?

DAVID. Yeah. Look, I got this killer idea for a screenplay. Takes place in Washington. All these white people are just like they're fucking nuts, okay, and there's this brother who sees everything, he's around all the time but nobody figures out that he's watching, and going, man, the country is fucked up, people suffering and dying on the streets, children with guns, it's like a war out there, and none of these fuckers see any of it, they're totally lost in this non-reality and it's like Anacosta or South East, different country man, they could give a shit, and every night this guy he's out there serving escargot, Puilly Fusses and Coque whatever to these people who are talking about taking food out of the mouths of children – like it's good *policy*, it's good *politics*.

And he's gotta be polite to these idiots. What do you think that does to somebody's *heart*? What do you *think*? *(Beat)* Anyway, this brother, the one watching them, he finally says fuck you, fuck you all, do your own fucking dishes, and then he blows up the white house.

E.T. BLACK. It's been done. *(Beat)* If you blew up the dome, that would work.

BARTENDER. Yeah, it could be the dome.

E.T. BLACK. Let's talk about this.

(He staggers off with the BARTENDER. EMMA calls after them.)

EMMA. But that's not how we started! It's not!

(ARTHUR enters, hopeful and excited.)

ARTHUR. I don't know. It's such a huge undertaking –

EMMA. Arthur, don't do this to me! It's taken me months to talk you into this, you can't back out now!

ARTHUR. I just think we should be realistic! I don't have a chance of winning –

EMMA. Come on, this is America. All sorts of idiots get elected to congress. If they can do it, you can too. Arthur! You've been talking about running as long as I've known you, and you're never going to get a better opportunity. I talked to my friend Tommy about you, he's been managing campaigns for a long time, not this high profile, but he knows the ropes. He says you have a shot. At least talk to him. Tommy!

ARTHUR. Tommy? Is this you young man?

VIEW OF THE DOME

EMMA. Sort of.
ARTHUR. "Sort of?"
EMMA. It's still early. But it's going well.

(TOMMY enters.)

TOMMY. So, is he going to do it?
EMMA. He's going to do it.
TOMMY. Excellent.

(EMMA and TOMMY kiss.)

ARTHUR. I didn't say that!
TOMMY. The party's in complete disarray, sir. The old standbys are terrified and well they should be. Everybody's looking for a dark horse. If you want to run, there's never going to be a better time.
ARTHUR. *(Considering)* And you can help me?
TOMMY. Yes, I can.
EMMA. Come on, Arthur. Wouldn't it be worse not to try? What's the worst that can happen?

(Beat)

ARTHUR. I'll do it.
EMMA. Yes!

(She and TOMMY kiss again. There is a brief celebratory moment as they all hug and congratulate each other.)

ARTHUR. *(To TOMMY, joking)* Now I have to call Natalie and tell her the bad news.

(He heads off. TOMMY calls after him.)

TOMMY. Get her down here! We can use all the help we can get! *(He goes. The mood changes. EMMA watches him as a BARTENDER crosses, pours him a drink and hands him the bottle.) (Cool, drinking)* Hello, Emma.
EMMA. Tommy.
TOMMY. I thought that was you.
EMMA. Hi.
TOMMY. Hi. *(Beat)* You're looking good.
EMMA. Thanks.
TOMMY. I mean, you look good. You just had a baby, right? I heard you had your baby.
EMMA. Six weeks ago.
TOMMY. Well, you look great.
EMMA. Thank you.
TOMMY. So, what'd you have?

(He pours himself a drink. She watches.)

EMMA. A boy.
TOMMY. Wow. That's great.
EMMA. Yes. It is.
TOMMY. So. Is it mine?

(Beat)

EMMA. No, actually. "It" is mine.
TOMMY. Yeah, that virgin birth stuff may have worked with your friends over in Christian la la land, but I happen to know better.

(He pours himself another drink.)

EMMA. You're drinking again.

TOMMY. How very observant of you. Yes, I have, for the moment, fallen off the wagon. It's temporary.

EMMA. It won't solve anything.

TOMMY. What would you know about it?

EMMA. Nothing. It's just, someone told me that.

TOMMY. Drinking doesn't solve anything. There's a news flash. I don't expect it to solve anything. I'm more interested in the way it blots things out.

EMMA. How's Arthur?

TOMMY. A little depressed. Losing kind of does that to you.

EMMA. He'll be fine.

TOMMY. Oh yeah. He was a newcomer, no one expected him to win. In fact, to tell you the truth, most people thought it was pretty impressive that he got as far as he did. A major scandal his first time out. The party boys took note. They want him to try again.

EMMA. Is that right?

TOMMY. *(Nodding)* Hoping for a liberal backlash. If the religious right hates him so much, he can't be all that bad, something like that. Annabeth thinks he's got a shot. Politicians, every last one of them, they're like this special breed of human beings made out of cork and Teflon ...

(He reaches for the bottle. EMMA tries to stop him.)

EMMA. Come on, Tommy –

(He moves it away from her.)

TOMMY. You could have returned my phone calls.

EMMA. I didn't see the point.

TOMMY. The baby is the point, Emma. The baby is the point.

EMMA. I just told you. It's not your kid.

TOMMY. Yeah, and I'm telling you. You're a big liar. I never thought you were. But then you got up, in front of the whole country and told the most spectacular set of fibs I ever heard. So I wouldn't stand there and act like just because words come out of your mouth we all have to believe them. I want to see the baby.

EMMA. That is not going to happen.

TOMMY. *(Furious)* I have a right. That is *my* son.

EMMA. *(Warning)* Tommy.

TOMMY. HE'S MY SON.

EMMA. Listen to me. He is not your son.

TOMMY. You just can't keep lying about this, Emma. Not about this.

EMMA. Like you're so honest. If you were so sure about this, why didn't you say something during the hearings? You had plenty of opportunities. You could have just slid it in between all those stories about how deranged I am.

TOMMY. I wasn't sure then. I'm sure now.

EMMA. That's convenient.

TOMMY. I didn't want to be involved!

EMMA. So, you got your wish.

TOMMY. You can't stop me. I'll demand a court order. I'll get paternity tests.

EMMA. *(Impatient)* No one is going to grant you parental rights. You come forward now, and everyone's going to think you collaborated in this fraud waged on the

U.S. Senate. Plus you're a big old alcoholic. I'm not afraid of you.
    TOMMY. *(Beat)* You're a cold bitch.
    EMMA. Fine.

(She stands to go. TOMMY grabs her arm to stop her. There is a very brief struggle. Embarrassed, he lets her go.)

    TOMMY. I'm sorry. *(He sits. She watches him.)* I guess none of us are who we thought we were, huh?
    EMMA. I guess not.
    TOMMY. Emma, please. What happened that one stupid night, it was so small, why can't you just let it go?
    EMMA. Look, you're the one who dumped me. Over nothing, over Arthur being a prick about seating arrangements. And now my child has no father. So don't tell me how small that evening was. That evening was not small.
    TOMMY. You should have told me about the baby –
    EMMA. I tried! But you could barely speak to me, remember? Arthur said to get rid of me, so you did. You didn't think twice. You didn't flinch.
    TOMMY. That's not how it was.
    EMMA. You couldn't throw me away fast enough.
    TOMMY. We all made mistakes.
    EMMA. Forget it. I got one good thing out of this whole mess, and I'm not going to screw it up. None of you people are coming near that kid. He is not your kid.
    TOMMY. You can't keep away the whole human race.
    EMMA. There are good people somewhere. I'll find them.
    TOMMY. You thought Arthur was good. You thought you were good. *(Beat)* Please. Let me see the baby.

EMMA. No.
TOMMY. You can't protect him.
EMMA. I have to go.

(She goes.)

TOMMY. YOU CAN'T PROTECT HIM!

(He slumps in his chair. EMMA looks at the audience.)

EMMA. You should see my boy. He's quite beautiful; he is, in fact, the most beautiful thing I've ever seen. My doctor tells me that the reason babies are so adorable is that if they weren't, we'd leave them by the side of the road. Which, I think, says more about us than it does about them. So how do you raise a child in a world that has people in it? How can I teach him to be good when I know that goodness will not protect him? I don't actually want to raise a little idealist; they turn into the most god-awful cynics. And I don't particularly want to watch his heart break when he learns what people are really like. But I look at him, and he is so clearly good, I don't know if I can bear to teach him anything else.
ANNABETH. Now, how do you want to do the seating, Arthur? Four and one?

(ARTHUR, ANNABETH, and TOMMY enter, taking their seats. EMMA looks over as ARTHUR considers this.)

ARTHUR. *(Quickly)* Oh, yes. That's exactly right. Four and one.
EMMA. And yet I fear the anger of the righteous.

ANNABETH. David – *(She waves the WAITER on.)* We'll need a table for four, and a table for one.

DAVID. Right this way.

(DAVID, the WAITER starts to move a place setting.)

TOMMY. Wait a minute. There are going to be five of us, aren't there? When the senator gets here –

EMMA. What's that quote about those small unremembered act of meanness that make up a man's life?

DAVID. Kindness. Small, unremembered acts of kindness.

EMMA. Are you sure?

ANNABETH. We'll set you up at the best single they have.

EMMA. I suppose the best I can do is to teach him to watch carefully. To struggle for objectivity. To believe always that the human spirit can and will transcend its own pettiness.

ANNABETH. David, can we get her the view of the capital dome?

DAVID. Anything for you, Annabeth.

EMMA. And when someone asks him to sit at another table ...

ARTHUR. Emma, you understand.

EMMA. He can go peacefully. Whole unto himself, without surrender.

ARTHUR. This is strictly business.

EMMA. *(To ARTHUR)* It's all right, Arthur. I prefer it over here. *(DAVID hands her a paperback.)* Thanks.

THE END

www.ingramcontent.com/pod-product-compliance
Lightning Source LLC
Chambersburg PA
CBHW072018290426
44109CB00018B/2279